START-UP
CITIZENSHIP

TAKING PART

Louise and Richard Spilsbury

Evans

Published by Evans Brothers Limited
2A Portman Mansions
Chiltern Street
London W1U 6NR

© Evans Brothers Limited 2007

Produced for Evans Brothers Limited by
White-Thomson Publishing Ltd.
Bridgewater Business Centre, 210 High Street,
Lewes, East Sussex BN7 2NH

Printed in China by WKT Co. Ltd.

Editor: Clare Collinson
Consultant: Roy Honeybone, Consultant in Citizenship
Education and Editor of *Teaching Citizenship*, the
journal of the Association for Citizenship Teaching
Designer: Leishman Design

British Library Cataloguing in Publication Data
Spilsbury, Louise
    Taking Part - (Start-up Citizenship)
    1. Social participation - Juvenile literature
    2. Interpersonal relations - Juvenile literature
    3. Citizenship - Juvenile literature
    I. Title II. Spilsbury, Richard, 1963-
    302.1'4

ISBN-13: 9780237532628

Acknowledgements:
Special thanks to the following for their help and
involvement in the preparation of this book: staff, pupils
and parents at Matchborough First School, Redditch,
Mount Carmel RC First School, Redditch and St
Stephens C of E First School, Redditch.

Picture Acknowledgements:
Alamy p. 4 (Elvele Images); Martyn Chillmaid pp. 6, 7
(both), 8, 9, 10, 11 (both), 12, 13, 14, 15 (all), 16, title
page and 17, 18, 19, 20r; iStockphoto.com p. 20l;
Yell.com pp. 5, 21.

Artwork:
Hattie Spilsbury, pp. 9, 11, 17.

Contents

Who takes part?

Taking part is important. At school we take part in many ways. We may answer questions in class, join in playtime games and help teachers to move chairs.

▶ These children are taking part in a school show. How do you take part in school life?

important   answer   help

We also take part in life at home and in our community. We may help with household chores or take part in decisions about a family trip.

▲ These children have been collecting old telephone books from people in their street. The books will be recycled. Why is it important to take part like this?

community   decisions   recycled   5

Speaking and listening

When should you speak and when should you listen when you take part in a conversation?

▶ Muna is reading her work to Dan. She speaks clearly. Dan listens carefully. Then he will say how he thinks Muna could improve her work.

What do you need to do to be a good speaker or a good listener?

speak   listen   conversation

In conversations, we use words to tell others how we feel. But it is not just our words that matter. We also use our eyes, hands and faces, for example when we smile or frown.

▲ Can you tell how these children feel? Do you think they are happy or sad? Are they angry or pleased?

feel   smile   frown

Join the circle!

Circle time is a chance to take part in discussions. This class is sharing ideas about friendship. The children take turns to say what they think makes a good friend.

▲ When someone holds the shell it is their turn to speak. Everyone else should listen. Which children are listening properly? What are the others doing wrong?

circle time   discussions   ideas

► **The class decides to make some rules for circle time for everyone to follow. They discuss and agree a list of rules. How do rules help us?**

Circle time rules

- wait your turn to speak

- Do not interrupt

- Tell the truth

- Do not hurt people's feelings

- Listen when someone else is talking

◄ **The children make a poster with their list of rules. Do you think these circle time rules are fair? What rules would you add to this list?**

rules   agree   poster

Making choices

This class is discussing school uniforms. Two older children from another school explain why their school has chosen not to wear a uniform.

Why is it good to hear other people's opinions?

uniforms   opinions

The class does a survey. They ask children, parents and teachers what they think about uniforms.

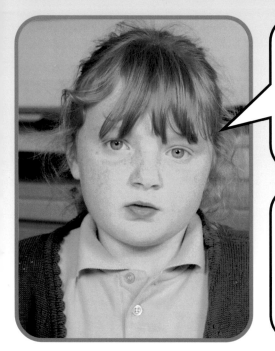

"I don't like uniforms. I want to wear my own clothes to school."

"Uniforms are a good idea because they help make children look smart."

◄ The children made a thought map to show their ideas. What would you add to a thought map like this?

survey   thought map

Solving problems

Sometimes there are problems at playtimes. What do you do if you want to play with a ball that someone else is using? What if someone will not share the bench?

◄ Tasha's friend is away from school today and no one else is playing with her. How do you think she feels?

What can we do to solve playground problems?

problems   solve

The children in Tasha's class work together to find ways to solve playground problems. They think of some new games that they can all play.

▲ In pairs the children take part in a role-play. Dan pretends to ask Zoe to play with him because she is all alone.

role-play   pretends

Setting up a school council

A **school council** is a group of children that take part in some school decisions. It is the job of each **member** to tell the council what their class thinks about a choice.

▶ Children here are **voting** for two people from their class to join the school council. What happens when people vote? Why do people write their votes in secret?

Votes for
school council
here

school council   member   voting

▼ **This poster shows the members of a school council. For each year there is one boy and one girl.**

Why is it important to have representatives **from every year? Why do you think this poster is** displayed **in the entrance hall of the school for everyone to see?**

representatives   displayed

Find out more

How do you find out about things you do not **understand**? To take part in decisions we may need to find out more before we make a choice.

► Dinners at this school are changing. The children in this class asked the school cook to come to talk to them. She tells them about her **plans** to make more **healthy** meals.

understand   plans   healthy

The class decides to do some research and find out about healthy foods.

◄ What different ways are these children using to research healthy foods?

► Jack designed this poster showing a healthy meal of vegetables and rice, a banana and a fruit milkshake. Why is it important to have a choice of healthy meals?

My Healthy Meal!

Making a difference

If we take part in decisions we can make a difference.

▲ There is going to be a new crossing on the road near Sam and Jess's school. How does this model they made help them think about where the crossing should go?

difference   crossing   model

▼ Sam discusses the new crossing with his group in class. The group decides to ask people in the community their views about where the crossing should go.

Sam and his group report back to the class. The class then writes to the town council to give the community's views on the decision.

report   council

Looking back

What can you learn from looking back at a decision or project you took part in?

"My class helped to choose new playground equipment. We learned to listen to what other people wanted too."

"At first I wanted a climbing frame. But other people voted for swinging log steps. I am happy with the log steps now."

project   learned

▼ Sometimes when we take part we get rewards afterwards. This school won a prize for collecting the most telephone books in a recycling competition.

Are rewards important? Why? Do we always need to get rewards?

rewards   competition   21

Further information for

New words listed in the text:

agree	decisions	help	plans	research	survey
answer	designed	ideas	poster	rewards	thought map
circle time	difference	important	pretends	role-play	understand
community	discussions	learned	problems	rules	uniforms
competition	displayed	listen	project	school council	voting
conversation	feel	member	recycled	smile	
council	frown	model	report	solve	
crossing	healthy	opinions	representatives	speak	

Possible Activities

PAGES 4-5

The children could make a list of the ways they take part at school, home and in clubs and the wider community. You could introduce the idea of responsibility. Sometimes we take part not because it is fun, as in a game of football, but because we have a responsibility to do so, for example when doing chores at home. What happens when you have a choice of things to take part in? How do you choose?

PAGES 6-7

Children could have fun pretending to be a 'bad' listener in role-play. One child tells a story while the other looks away, makes a noise, moves around etc. Then the other children in the class spot what the listener is doing wrong. In pairs children could practise listening skills. One could give a list of things they like and the other, after listening carefully, could write down or draw as many of those things as they can remember. To help them understand how body language and facial expressions work, they could work in groups to mime different feelings and let other groups guess what they mean.

PAGES 8-9

A discussion about a list of rules is a chance to get the children to brainstorm a number of alternatives and consider their options before discussing and agreeing a final list. This encourages them to discuss and listen to other people's ideas and to compromise. This could be done with a set of class rules for the playground. The children could even discuss what order of importance to put these rules in. Do they think they are all equally important?

PAGES 10-11

It is useful for children to research and discuss a real-life issue that affects them and their school. It could be something to do with playtimes, dinners or mixing with older children. You could introduce the word 'debate' and encourage them to let other people make a point before making their own point and to treat other people's opinions with respect. In groups the class

Parents and Teachers

could discuss a topical issue and choose a spokesperson from each group to report back to the whole class.

PAGES 12-13
In PE children could work together to devise a new playground game (or find out about one that is new to them) that everyone could play and then make an instruction card about it. This might also be a chance to invite an older member of the community to talk about playground games in the past and explain how some of them were played.

PAGES 14-15
Ideally school councils should evolve from circle time and class councils so children understand the idea of discussions and joint decision-making before they vote for or join a school council. Discuss the importance of voting in secret so you are able to give a choice without being influenced by other people (as compared to voting by a show of hands). They could also discuss why the poster in this book has one boy and one girl from each year. Is this fair? Should people only be allowed to stay on a school council for a limited time?

PAGES 16-17
Children should research using a variety of methods but having someone talk to them is also good for listening skills. For discussions about healthy eating, a school nurse, local doctor, local authority advisor for PSHE or a supervisor from the school meals service could be invited to school. To extend this work, children could also think about the cost limitations involved when planning school meals and the problems of creating healthy menus that will appeal to everyone and take in everyone's preferences.

Further Information

BOOKS FOR CHILDREN
An Eco-school (Taking Part series) by Sally Hewitt (Franklin Watts, 2002)

A Pupil Parliament (Taking Part series) by Sally Hewitt (Franklin Watts, 2002)

Caring for the Environment (Making a Difference series) by Jillian Powell (Hodder Wayland, 1997)

WEBSITES
http://www.childline.org.uk
http://www.csv.org.uk
http://www.schoolcouncils.org.uk

PAGES 18-19
In groups the children could work on a topic, either real or imaginary, to come up with a list of questions. One child could be chair and lead the discussion; another could act as scribe and take notes. The groups should come up with five questions they could ask in a survey. They will have to consider and choose from alternatives and negotiate a final list together.

PAGES 20-21
After taking part in a discussion about a choice in groups, the children could report back on how well the group worked. Did people listen to each other? How did they negotiate their final choices? The children could also think about incentives and rewards. These can be useful, but it is also important to discuss the idea of taking part for the sake of taking part, because it is our duty and responsibility.

Index